CEDAR MILL COMM LIBRARY
12505 NW CORNELL RD
PORTLAND, OR 97229
(503) 644-0043

WITHDRAWN
CEDAR MILL LIBRARY

D0578211

EDGE BOOKS™

Imagine It, Build It

-Incredible-

DUCT TAPE PROJECTS

You Can Create

by Marne Ventura

CAPSTONE PRESS
a capstone imprint

Edge Books are published by Capstone Press,
1710 Roe Crest Drive, North Mankato, Minnesota 56003
www.capstonepub.com

Copyright © 2016 by Capstone Press, a Capstone imprint. All rights reserved. No part of
this publication may be reproduced in whole or in part, or stored in a retrieval system, or
transmitted in any form or by any means, electronic, mechanical, photocopying, recording,
or otherwise, without written permission of the publisher.

Library of Congress Cataloging-in-Publication Data
Ventura, Marne, author.
Incredible duct tape projects you can create / by Marne Ventura.
pages cm.—(Edge books. Imagine it, build it)
Summary: "Simple step-by-step instructions teach readers how to make original projects
from duct tape"—Provided by publisher.
Audience: Ages 8–12
Audience: Grades 4 to 6
Includes bibliographical references.
ISBN 978-1-4914-4290-6 (library binding)
ISBN 978-1-4914-4326-2 (eBook PDF)
1. Tape craft—Juvenile literature. 2. Duct tape—Juvenile literature. I. Title.
TT869.7.V46 2016
745.5—dc23   2015001413

Editorial Credits
Aaron Sautter, editor; Richard Korab, designer; Ted Williams, art director; Sarah Schuette,
studio stylist; Marcy Morin, studio scheduler; Laura Manthe, production specialist

Photo Credits
All photographs by Capstone Studio: Karon Dubke

Design Elements
iStockphoto: studio9400; Shutterstock: Alhovik, Luminis, M.E. Mulder, Ronald Sumners

Printed in the United States of America in North Mankato, Minnesota.
062015   008823CGF15

TABLE OF CONTENTS

Create Incredible Duct Tape Projects!......... 4

Awesome Laser Sword 6

Super Tri-Fold Wallet 9

Cool, Colorful Kite.........................12

Easy Travel Checkers Set...................16

Pirate Booty Treasure Chest 18

Sports Team Ball Cap......................21

Hot Beats Bongo Drums 24

Incredible Superhero Helmet 26

#1 Sports Fan Glove 29

Read More..................32
Internet Sites..............32

Create Incredible Duct Tape Projects!

It's strong, flexible, waterproof, and super sticky. People use it to fix everything from windows and boats to baseball bats. Some people even use it to make warts disappear. What is this awesome stuff? It's duct tape!

First made from sticky cotton fabric, soldiers once used this tape to seal boxes of ammunition. Duct tape later got its name when builders used it to hold the joints of ducts together. This amazing tape is great for fixing things, but it's also a popular craft supply. It comes in many colors and patterns and can be used to make all sorts of cool projects.

Grab a couple rolls of duct tape and get ready to make awesome laser swords, superhero helmets, and many other incredible projects!

Tips and Tricks

» Get a good cutting mat. Craft stores sell mats with grid lines that help make measuring easy. A wood or plastic cutting board and a ruler will also work well.

» Before starting a project, read through all of the steps and be sure to gather all the necessary materials.

» When building something long, it works best to cut shorter strips of tape and then join them together.

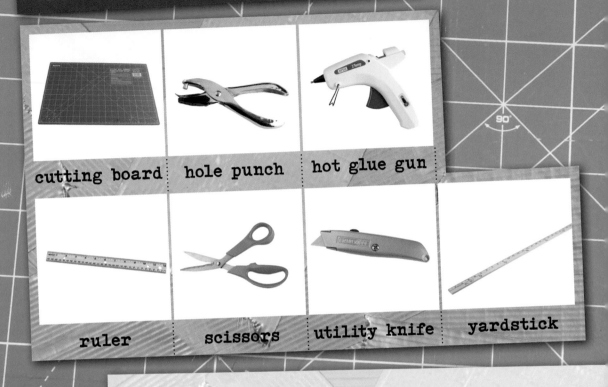

cutting board | hole punch | hot glue gun

ruler | scissors | utility knife | yardstick

Duct Tape Fabric

Some projects are made with duct tape fabric. To make this, first lay a strip of duct tape face up on your work surface. Then add a second strip by overlapping the long edge 0.25 inch (0.6 centimeters). Repeat this with more strips of tape until the fabric is wide enough. Then place strips of tape sticky-side-down to cover the first layer.

5

Awesome Laser Sword

Heading out to battle evil aliens? Smart space warriors never leave home without their trusty laser sword. With some colorful duct tape and cardboard tubes, you can make one of your own! Fight intergalactic battles with friends, or you can add a hooded cape for a cool Halloween costume.

MATERIALS

- 40-inch (102-cm) long cardboard giftwrap tube
- 9-inch (23-cm) long cardboard paper towel tube
- two 12- by 12-inch (30- by 30-cm) squares of aluminum foil
- glow-in-the-dark duct tape
- silver duct tape
- black duct tape
- red duct tape

Step 1: First crumple one square of aluminum foil into a ball about as wide as the long tube. Use hot glue to secure the foil ball halfway inside the end of the tube.

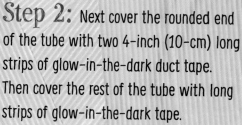

Step 2: Next cover the rounded end of the tube with two 4-inch (10-cm) long strips of glow-in-the-dark duct tape. Then cover the rest of the tube with long strips of glow-in-the-dark tape.

Step 3: Crumple the second square of foil into a ball. Hot glue it to one end of the short tube. Cover the round end with two 4-inch (10-cm) long strips of silver duct tape. Then cover the length of this tube with silver duct tape.

Step 4: Cut two or three 5-inch (13-cm) long strips of black duct tape in various widths. Use these to add stripes to the short tube.

Step 5: Tape four small squares of red duct tape onto the tube to make buttons, switches, and controls.

Step 6: Slide the short tube onto the open end of the long tube. If it doesn't fit snugly, use hot glue to keep it in place. Now you're ready to save the galaxy!

Tip: Try giving your laser sword 3-D buttons, switches, and controls. Use hot glue to attach craft foam cutouts to the handle. Then cover them with squares of colored duct tape.

Super Tri-Fold Wallet

Would you like a colorful, waterproof wallet that shows your personality? This cool wallet can be made from your favorite colors. Or you can even create your own superhero logo. Use it to safely stash your cash before taking off to save the world.

MATERIALS

- silver duct tape
- green duct tape
- white duct tape
- black duct tape
- clear plastic freezer bag

Step 1: Make two pieces of 4- by 10-inch (10- by 25-cm) silver duct tape fabric. (See page 5 for directions on making duct tape fabric.)

....

Step 2: Lay the two pieces on top of each other. Fold a 10-inch (25-cm) long strip of duct tape over the bottom to join the two pieces together. Then fold a 4-inch (10-cm) long strip of duct tape over each side to join the two sides. Leave the wallet open on top.

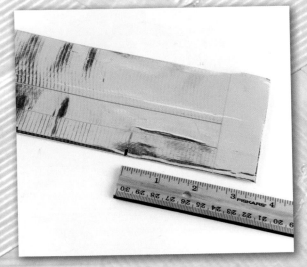

Step 3: Lay a ruler along the bottom of the wallet. With a pen or pencil, make a mark a little less than 3.5 inches (9 cm) from the left side. Make another mark about 3.5 inches (9 cm) from the right side. Fold the right side of the wallet in to make a crease. Do the same on the left side. Place a heavy book on the wallet to squeeze the creases tighter. Leave the book on the wallet for at least one hour.

Step 4: Make two more pieces of duct tape fabric measuring 2 by 3.75 inches (5 by 9.5 cm). Measure and mark 1 inch (2.5 cm) from the right edge of the wallet. Attach the right side of one fabric piece at the mark with a 0.5-inch (1.3-cm) wide strip of tape.

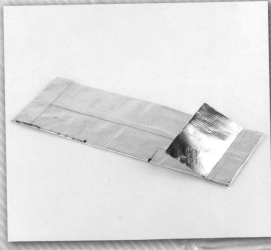

10

Step 5: Place the second fabric piece on top of the first. Line up the right side with the right edge of the wallet. Use 0.5-inch (1.3-cm) wide strips of tape to attach the fabric pieces at the top, bottom, and right edges. Leave the left sides open to form pockets for the wallet.

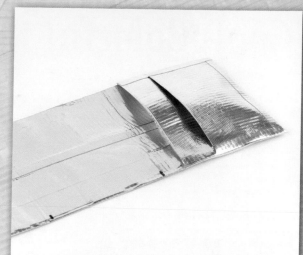

Step 6: Repeat steps 4 and 5 on the left third of the wallet.

Step 7: Cut a rectangle measuring 2.5 by 3.75 inches (6 by 9.5 cm) from the plastic bag. Fold a 0.5-inch (1.3-cm) wide strip of tape over one long edge of the plastic. Use more strips of tape to attach the plastic to the center of the wallet. Leave the top edge open to create a clear pocket.

Step 8: Cut your first initial or a superhero logo from green duct tape. Stick the logo onto white duct tape and cut around the shape to create a border. Stick this piece onto a black circle. Stick the circle to the front to finish your wallet.

Tip: You could also try using your favorite sports team's colors and logo for your wallet.

Cool, Colorful Kite

What do Benjamin Franklin and Charlie Brown have in common? They both flew kites! Become a member of the kite flyers club by making your own duct tape kite. Use bright colors to make your kite stand out against the blue sky.

MATERIALS

- 1/8-inch (0.3-cm) wide dowel, 36 inches (91 cm) long
- 1/8-inch (0.3-cm) wide dowel, 33 inches (84 cm) long
- black marker
- large spool of strong string
- colorful duct tape
- large plastic garbage bag

Step 1: Measure 10 inches (25 cm) from the top of the longer dowel and make a mark. Measure and mark the exact center of the shorter dowel.

Step 2: Place the dowels together where they are marked to form a "T" shape. Cut a 12-inch (30.5-cm) long piece of the string. Start 3 inches (8 cm) from the end of the string and wind it around the point where the dowels cross. Tightly wind the string around both dowels in a repeating "X" pattern. Tightly tie the two ends of the string together. To make the connection extra sturdy, wrap a small piece of duct tape around the string.

Step 3: Cut two sides of the garbage bag so it is a single sheet of plastic. Lay the kite frame on the sheet of plastic. Draw a kite shape around it with the marker. Leave a 1-inch (2.5-cm) wide margin beyond the ends of the dowels.

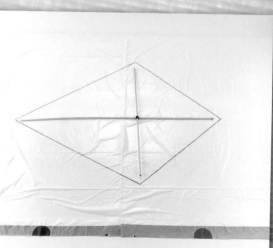

Step 4: Turn over the plastic sheet. Cover the plastic where the kite shape is drawn with strips of duct tape. Be sure to overlap the strips by 0.25 inch (0.6 cm).

Step 5: Flip the plastic over again. Cut out the kite shape. Lay the kite frame on the kite and tape the dowels in place. Fold in the margin around the edges of the kite and over the ends of the dowels. Tape the edges down with small strips of duct tape. Make the corners neat by folding them in before folding in the sides.

Step 6: On the horizontal dowel, make marks 6 inches (15 cm) from the vertical dowel on each side. Punch small holes through the kite at both marks.

Step 7: Tie the end of a 28-inch (71-cm) long piece of string to the horizontal dowel at one mark. Thread the string through the holes in the kite. Tie the other end of the string to the horizontal dowel at the second mark.

Step 8: Cut an 18-inch (46-cm) long piece of duct tape in half lengthwise. Stick the end of one piece onto the second to make a 36-inch (91-cm) long piece. Fold the tape in half lengthwise to make a tail.

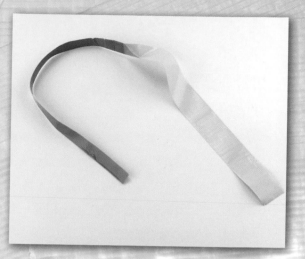

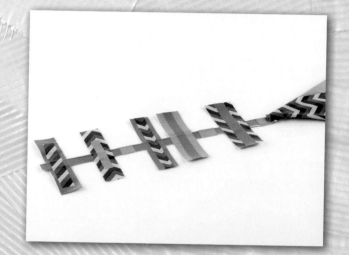

Step 9: Cut six 6-inch (15-cm) long pieces of duct tape in half lengthwise. Place them on the tail 5 inches (13 cm) apart with the tail sandwiched between them. Then tape the tail to the bottom of the kite.

Step 10: Tie the spool of flying string to the center of the front string on the kite. Now find a wide open, windy space to fly your new kite!

Easy Travel Checkers Set

Need something fun to do on a long car trip? Turn a clean pizza box into a cool checkers set before you hit the road. The checkerboard doubles as a lid, and you can store the playing pieces inside the box. You could even throw some playing cards and a good book in there too!

MATERIALS

- clean 10- by 10-inch (25- by 25-cm) pizza box
- black duct tape
- red duct tape
- 24 water bottle caps

Step 1: Cut a 14-inch (36-cm) long strip of red duct tape. Fold it in half lengthwise with the sticky sides together. Repeat this step to make eight red strips and eight black strips.

Step 2: Lay the eight strips of red tape side-by-side on a flat surface. Use a strip of tape to hold them down on one end. Now weave the black strips through the red strips to form a checkerboard.

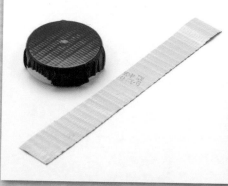

Step 3: Place red tape on the sides of the checkerboard to hold everything in place. Trim each side so it's 1 inch (2.5 cm) wider than the checkerboard.

Step 4: Use red tape to attach the checkerboard to the top of the pizza box. Use black tape to cover the sides of the pizza box.

Step 5: Next cut 1- by 1-inch (2.5- by 2.5-cm) squares of duct tape. Make 12 red squares and 12 black squares. Stick the squares to the tops of the bottle caps and smooth the corners down. Cut 0.25- by 4-inch (0.6- by 10-cm) strips of red and black duct tape. Use these to cover the sides of the caps. Trim off any excess tape. Store the checkers inside the box.

Pirate Booty Treasure Chest

Aarrr! Shiver me timbers!
Every pirate needs a safe place to
store secret loot. Keep land lovers
from snooping into your stuff with
this duct tape treasure chest. Add
a skull and crossbones or "KEEP
OUT" sign so curious siblings
know you mean business.

MATERIALS

- plain cardboard box
  with hinged lid
- wood grain duct tape
- black duct tape
- brass fasteners
- large washer
- small padlock

Step 1: Cover the box and lid with wood grain duct tape.

Step 2: Use black duct tape to cover the edges of the box. Make a black stripe down the center of the box as well.

Step 3: Measure and make several evenly spaced marks along the black stripes. Punch small holes into the box at each mark.

Step 4: Push a brass fastener into each hole. On the inside of the box, bend the ends of the fasteners out flat.

Tip: If you can't find a box with a hinged lid, you can use a regular shoe box with a lid. Cut away the overhang on one long side of the lid. Then attach it to the box with black duct tape.

Step 5: Make a 1-inch (2.5-cm) long mark at the front center of the box, just under the lid. Cut a slit at this mark to insert the washer.

Step 6: Cover the washer with black duct tape. Leave the hole open in the middle. Use hot glue to attach the washer in place inside the box.

Step 7: Make a 2- by 3-inch (5- by 7.5-cm) piece of black duct tape fabric. Cut a slit in the piece to fit over the washer on the front of the box. Attach this piece inside the front center of the lid. Now just add your secret loot and lock it up to keep it safe!

Sports Team Ball Cap

Heading to the ballpark? Don't forget your duct tape cap! Choose duct tape that matches your team's colors. Then add a logo to make your cap stand out in the crowd.

MATERIALS

- 1 old cap with a bill
- cardstock
- pen
- plastic grocery bags
- aluminum foil
- duct tape in your favorite team's colors

Step 1: Trace the bill of the cap onto a piece of cardstock. Cut out the cardboard bill.

Step 2: Adjust the cap to fit your head. Then stuff the inside of the cap with crumpled plastic bags to hold it's shape. Mold a large sheet of aluminum foil over the top of the cap. Fold the edges to the inside.

Step 3: Cover the foil with 2-inch (5-cm) squares of duct tape. Overlap and smooth the squares to completely cover the foil. The edges of the duct tape should go a little beyond the edges of the hat.

Step 4: Turn the hat upside down and remove the plastic bags. Unfold the foil from the edges of the hat and gently pull the hat away from the foil.

Step 5: Use a few bits of tape to attach the cardstock bill to the inside of the foil.

Step 6: Cover the bill and the inside of the hat with 2-inch (5-cm) squares of overlapping duct tape.

Step 7: Cut out a duct tape team logo and add it to the front of the cap. Now you're ready to cheer on your favorite team in style!

Tip: To make a slightly smaller cap, begin by molding the foil to the inside of the cap instead of the outside.

Hot Beats Bongo Drums

Every band needs a drummer! Use this set of bongo drums to play some great music with your friends. Tap the drums with your fingertips and the palms of your hands. Or for a different sound, try using drumsticks or chopsticks.

MATERIALS
- 1 medium oatmeal container
- 1 large oatmeal container
- white, tan, and black duct tape
- brass fasteners
- small block of wood,
    2 by 1.5 by 1.5 inches
    (5 by 3.8 by 3.8 cm)

Step 1: Remove the lids and turn the containers upside down. Cover the bottoms of the containers with white duct tape. Cut strips long enough to cross the center and overlap the sides of the containers about 1 inch (2.5 cm). Cover the sides of the drums with vertical stripes of tan and black duct tape.

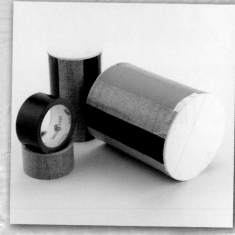

Step 2: Cut a strip of white tape long enough to fit around the drum with a 2-inch (5-cm) overlap. Fold it in half lengthwise with the sticky sides together. Make two strips for each drum.

Step 3: Measure and mark about 1.5 inches (3.8 cm) from the top and bottom edges of each drum. Attach the white strips at the marks with a bit of tape. Punch small holes through the white strip and the drum at the center of each tan stripe. Push brass fasteners through the holes. Flatten the fasteners inside the drums.

Step 4: Cover the block of wood with a piece of black duct tape. Hot glue the two drums on each side of the wood block. Now you're ready to lay down some awesome beats!

Tip: Coffee cans and cornmeal containers make good drums too. For the best sound, leave the bottom of the drum open.

Incredible Superhero Helmet

Want to be a superhero? What would your super power be? Flying? Super speed? Leaping over skyscrapers? Whatever it is, you can show it off with your own personal duct tape superhero helmet!

MATERIALS

- duct tape in your favorite colors
- plastic grocery bag
- sturdy foam head stand

Step 1: Cut several 5-inch (13-cm) long strips of duct tape and several 2-inch (5-cm) squares of duct tape. Place the tape on a cutting board so they're ready to use.

Step 2: Fit the grocery bag over the foam head stand. Cut away the plastic so it covers the hair and forehead areas, but not the face. (Safety note: Plastic bags can be dangerous. Never place a plastic bag over your own head or anyone else's head.)

Step 3: Cover the plastic bag with the strips of duct tape.

Step 4: Cut a mask out of the leftover plastic to go over the eyes and top of the nose. Cut out eyeholes in the mask.

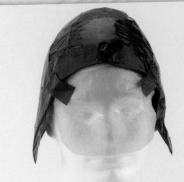

Step 5: Tape the mask to the front of the helmet at the sides.

Step 6: Cover the plastic mask with small strips of duct tape in a different color. Trim the edges of the helmet into whatever shape you want.

Step 7: It's time to personalize! You can add duct tape initials, logos, or numbers to the sides of the helmet. Use your imagination to create the coolest helmet you can think of. When you're done, put on your helmet and head out to save the world!

Tip: Cut out cardboard shapes and cover them with duct tape to make horns or antennae. Then tape them to the top of the helmet.

#1 Sports Fan Glove

Do you love those giant hands that people wave around at sporting events? You can make your own in your favorite team's colors from bubble wrap and duct tape. Take this to the next game to show your team spirit.

MATERIALS

- 2 sheets of cardstock 8.5 by 11 inches (22 by 28 cm)
- clear tape
- pen or marker
- 4 sheets of bubble wrap, about 10 by 18 inches (25 by 46 cm)
- double-sided tape
- duct tape in your favorite team's colors

29

Step 1: Tape the long sides of two sheets of cardstock together with clear tape.

....

Step 2: Draw a large hand on the cardstock. Make it with the number 1 finger pointing up. Cut out the hand to use for a pattern.

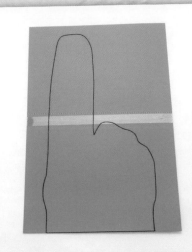

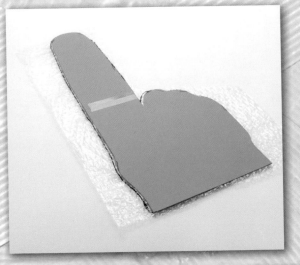

Step 3: Trace the pattern onto the four sheets of bubble wrap. Cut the hands out.

Step 4: Tape two of the bubble wrap hands together with double-sided tape. Repeat for the other two hands. Then lay the two sets of hands on top of one another.

....

Step 5: Cut several strips of duct tape 2 to 3 inches (5 to 7.6 cm) longer than the width of the hands.

Step 6: Fold a strip of duct tape over the bottom edge of the top layer of hands. Place it so that half of the strip goes inside the glove. Repeat this step with the bottom layer of hands.

Step 7: Cover the outside of the glove with duct tape. Fold the strips of tape around the edges to hold the layers of bubble wrap together. Overlap the edges of the duct tape for a smooth finish.

Step 8: Add a large "#1" to the front of the glove in a different color of duct tape. Now go cheer your team on to victory!

Tip: You can find sheets of bubble wrap in shipping supply sections of department stores.

Read More

Bell-Rehwoldt, Sheri. *The Kids' Guide to Duct Tape Projects.* Kids' Guides. Mankato, Minn.: Capstone Press, 2012.

Erickson, Steven. *The Beginner Book.* Warfare by Duct Tape. Thomaston, Ga.: Chinquapin Press, LLC, 2014.

Goldrich Wolf, Laurie. *Boy-Made.* Green and Groovy Crafts. New York: Downtown Bookworks, 2012.

Morgan, Richela Fabian. *Tape It and Make It: 101 Duct Tape Activities.* Hauppauge, N.Y.: Barron's, 2012.

Internet Sites

FactHound offers a safe, fun way to find Internet sites related to this book. All of the sites on FactHound have been researched by our staff.

Here's all you do:

Visit *www.facthound.com*

Type in this code: 9781491442906

Super-cool stuff! Check out projects, games and lots more at **www.capstonekids.com**